How to Host Your Website

It's Your Business Address

Book 4 in the Internet Marketing FAST Series

Copyright and Enquiries

Contents

How to Host Your Website

It's Your Business Address

How to Host Your Website

It's Your Business Address

Table of Figures

How to Host Your Website

It's Your Business Address

How to Host Your Website

It's Your Business Address

Open a Web Host Account

What is a Website Host?

Figure 1: Web Hosting and Domain Hosting

A website host is a computer connected to the internet where your website is stored. When someone enters your website's domain name into a search engine, the search engine retrieves your website's details from the website host and displays them.

Domain Name Host

A domain name host like Namecheap holds all of the details of your new domain name and most importantly, translates the human-readable address domainname.com into the actual digital address where your website is stored. This is referred to as your DNS (Domain Name Server).

Web Host

Domain Name Hosts will frequently offer web hosting as well.

How to Host Your Website

I really prefer to keep the two separate and independent. And, as you will see, I'm about to recommend a solution that provides fast web hosting for free, along with a heap of other benefits.

Wealthy Affiliate

Figure 2: What Wealthy Affiliate Offers

I cannot recommend Wealthy Affiliate highly enough.

It's not just a website host. In fact, that's almost just an incidental by-product of what they offer.

Wealthy Affiliate is a 400,000+ world-wide community of successful and aspiring internet marketers.

And you can join for FREE!

How to Host Your Website

It's Your Business Address

Join Wealthy Affiliate for FREE here

Wealthy Affiliate has the most comprehensive, step by step training that you will find anywhere on the internet.

In fact, if you follow each step of the training and implement it as you go, you are pretty much guaranteed success.

And if you are stuck at any time or just need help or clarification, just post a question and a member of the WA community will answer it for you. In fact, often several members and, because it's a world-wide community, often more or less instantly.

What Does Wealthy Affiliate Cost?

There are two levels of membership, Free and Premium.

There is no trial period. You can stay a free member for ever, if you wish.

Premium membership costs $19 for the first month and then $49 per month thereafter. For what you get, it's the bargain of your internet marketing lifetime. If only one of your websites made just $2 per day, you'd have your cost covered.

It's even less if you pay 6 months or 12 months up front. $234 for 6 months ($39 per month) or $359 for 12 months ($29.92 per month).

What Do You Get with Wealthy Affiliate?

It's kind of hard to summarize it all to an outsider looking in, but once on the inside it quickly becomes apparent that it far exceeds anything else that is out there on the web.

- It starts with state-of-the-art website security for all sites hosted at WA.

How to Host Your Website

It's Your Business Address

- Complete site backup every 24 hours for all sites, protecting against a site owner's worst nightmare ... site crash.
- Premium membership includes unlimited searches using the powerful Jaaxy keyword search tool, which shows not only the number of searches for different keyword variations, but also the amount of competition. You can also use Jaaxy to see where your site is ranking on Google, Bing and Yahoo.
- Then there's the extraordinary features of Wealthy Affiliate's SiteRubix portal which almost defy complete description. It is the most technologically advanced website facility on the web and it's included with Premium membership. This is where your websites will be hosted.
- The Site Feedback feature gets valuable feedback from the community helping you to improve and optimize your sites. The Site Comment feature allows you to trade comments on other members' sites for comments on your own, thereby increasing engagement, which is a major factor for Google to determine site ranking.
- Incredibly responsive and accurate website Tech Support for fixing site anomalies and problems. Forget outsourced help desks, this is the real deal.
- The most comprehensive and up to date Affiliate Marketing training on the web ... world class does not adequately describe it.
- The most supportive community of like-minded folks providing almost instantaneous 1 on 1 coaching. It's the most interactive, helpful, and engaging online business building platform in the world. "It's More Than Anything Out There. It's Wealthy Affiliate."

And the best part is it just keeps getting better and better thanks to Kyle and Carson's commitment to continuous improvement.

How to Host Your Website

It's Your Business Address

Here's a summary of the differences between Free and Premium membership. And remember, YOU choose when to go premium (if at all). The Free membership gives you plenty of features and enough time to decide if Wealthy Affiliate is for you.

How to Host Your Website

It's Your Business Address

WealthyAffiliate.com Membership Options	Starter For Newbies to Get Started Fast! $0/month	Premium For Those Who are READY for Success! $49/month
Live Help	First 7 Days	Unlimited
Private Messaging	✖	✔
Websites	2 Websites	50 Websites
Website Security Package	✖	✔
Website Backup	✔	✔
Beginner Training Course	✔	✔
Personal Affiliate Blog	✔	✔
Affiliate Bootcamp Training	Phase 1	All Phases (7)
Live Video Classes	✖	✔
Video Walk-Throughs	✔	✔
Keyword Research Tool	30 Searches	Unlimited Searches
Training Classrooms	2	12
Affiliate Program	✔	2x Higher Payout
Earn While You Learn	✔	✔
1-on-1 Coaching	First 7 Days	Unlimited
Private Access to Owners	✖	✔
24/7/365 Website Support	✖	✔
Website Feedback Platform	✖	✔
Website Comment Platform	✖	✔
Website Analysis	✖	✔
Best For	Getting Started $0.00	Those Ready to Earn! $49.00

Create Your Account Today!

Figure 3: Wealthy Affiliate Membership Options

How to Host Your Website

It's Your Business Address

Wealthy Affiliate: Not Your Average Web Host

I hope you can see why I recommend WA to host your web sites. For the same price or less than some companies charge to do nothing but host your website, Wealthy Affiliate gives you so much more. In fact, everything you need, including the training, to be a successful internet marketer.

Join Wealthy Affiliate HERE

I'm an affiliate of WA as well as an enthusiastic user. If you join through my link and subsequently upgrade to a Premium membership, I will get paid a commission. This doesn't affect your cost at all. But you will have me as your personal mentor. I'm ranked in the top 50 of WA's 400,000+ members. Ranking is based on knowledge and ability to help others in the WA community.

You can go to Wealthy Affiliate HERE.

SiteGround

The main advantages of Wealthy Affiliate are the video training, the community support and the keyword research. The fact that you can host your websites there is a side benefit.

If you don't feel the need for additional training, or simply don't wish to pay Wealthy Affiliate's fees, I recommend using SiteGround as your web host. They use fast, 100% reliable servers and their support is excellent.

What Does SiteGround Cost?

SiteGround has three service levels and corresponding pricing.

How to Host Your Website

It's Your Business Address

Startup

The Startup plan allows you to host one website and costs $4.95 per month, billed as $59.40 for 12 months. You can have up to 10,000 website visitors per month.

I don't recommend this, as you will want to build several internet marketing businesses, not just one. In addition, the higher plans offer more features.

GrowBig

The GrowBig plan allows you to host an unlimited number of websites and provides premium features. It costs $7.45 a month, billed as $89.40 for 12 months. You can have up to 25,000 website visitors per month.

This is the plan I recommend that you use. It will allow you to get several businesses up and running on a fast, reliable server at an economic price.

GoGeek

The GoGeek plan is for when you have a large number of businesses running and want the best possible facilities for them. It costs $14.95 a month, billed as $179.40 for 12 months. It caters for up to 100,000 visitors a month.

You'll know when you're ready for this!

What Do You Get with SiteGround?

- The fastest, most reliable web host servers available on the internet
- Choice of server location. Choose the ones geographically closest to your target market for the fastest load time possible
- Free SSL certificate for all your websites, so that they use https protocol, essential for Google trust

How to Host Your Website

It's Your Business Address

- One-click WordPress installation
- The best support in the business.

To sign up with SiteGround, or just to find out more, go to Check SiteGround Here.

How to Host Your Website
It's Your Business Address

Pointing Your Domain Name to Your Host's DNS

When someone enters your domain name into a web browser like Google or Bing, it has to find your web host to bring up your website. Your web host and your domain name host must be linked.

This is achieved by entering your web host's DNS (Domain Name Servers) into your domain name details at your domain name host's website. This is a one-time job.

If you used Namecheap as recommended for your domain name host, this is how you do it.

Sign into Namecheap

Sign into Namecheap using the credentials you established when you registered your domain name(s).

How to Host Your Website

It's Your Business Address

Figure 4: Sign in to Namecheap

Then click on *Domain List*.

How to Host Your Website

It's Your Business Address

Figure 5: Click on Domain List

How to Host Your Website

It's Your Business Address

Select the Domain to be Updated

Click the check box next to the domain name to be edited then the drop-down labelled *Actions* and select *DNS / Host Records*.

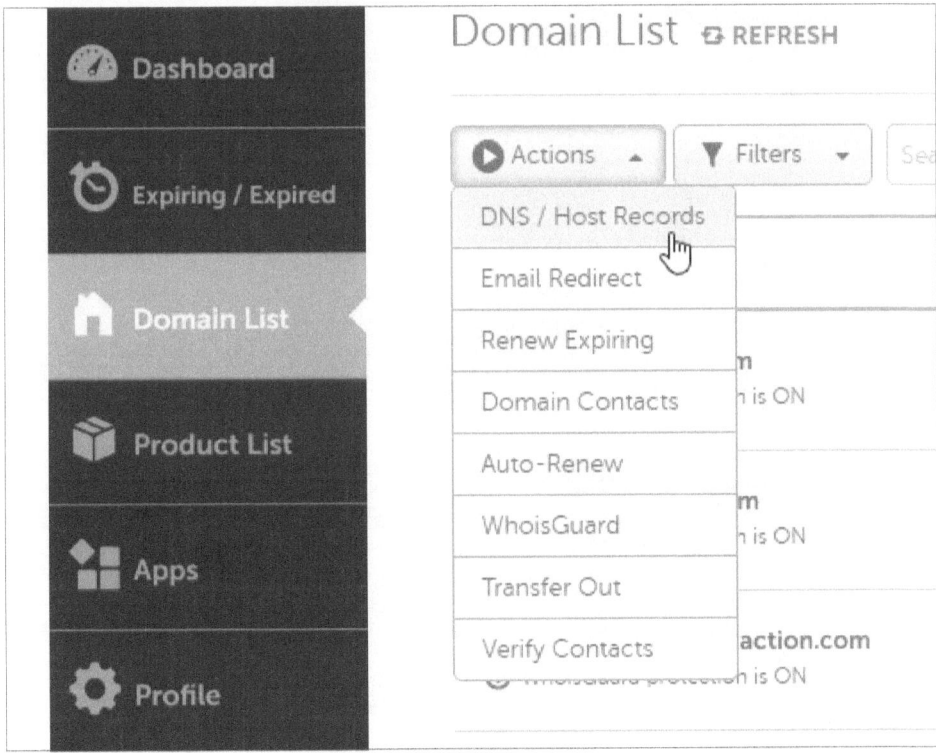

Figure 6: Select the Domain Name to be Updated

On the next screen, click the check boxes that say you know what you're doing and then the **Next** button.

Enter Your Web Host's Name Servers

Check the radio button Custom DNS and enter your web host's domain name servers. If you are using <u>Wealthy Affiliate</u> as your web host, these will be ns1.mywahosting.com and ns2.mywahosting.com. If

How to Host Your Website
It's Your Business Address

you are using SiteGround, they will have advised you of the DNS to be used for your chosen plan and location.

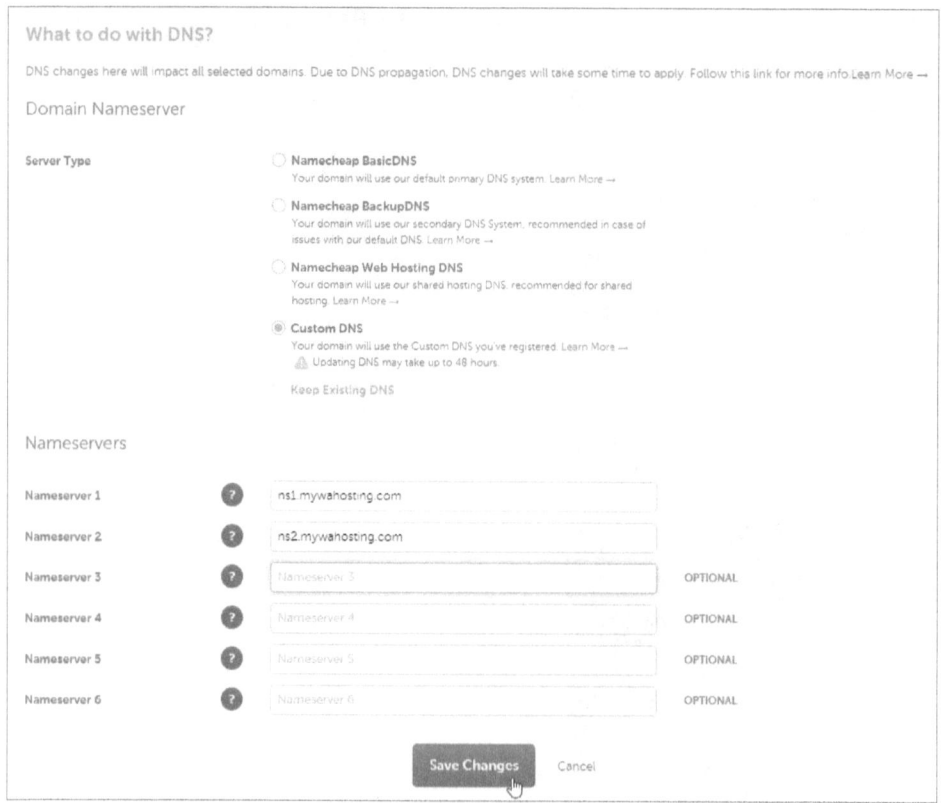

Figure 7: Update the Name Servers

Save and Propagate

Then click on *Save Changes*.

Note that this doesn't happen immediately because there are servers all over the world that need to be updated. This is called propagation. Although you will be told to allow up to 48 hours, it normally only takes a few hours.

20

How to Host Your Website

It's Your Business Address

If you are not using Namecheap as your domain name host, the procedure will be different, but the principle is the same. Similarly, if you are not using Wealthy Affiliate or SiteGround as your web host, the name servers will also be different.

How to Host Your Website

It's Your Business Address

How to Transfer a Website

There are a number of ways to transfer a website from one web host to another.

My preference is to use a reliable backup and restore plugin.

You create a backup file at your old host and use it to restore your site at your new host.

This has the very real advantage of not committing you. If something goes wrong with the process, you still have your old website. You won't delete your old site until you know that the new one is running perfectly.

A transfer to SiteGround is used as an example here.

Before You Start

Backup the Old Website

Backup the website at the server where it is now using the All-in-One WP Migration WordPress plugin.

See Book 5 in my Internet Marketing FAST series *WordPress for the Technically Challenged* for details but here is a quick overview.

Install the All in One WP Migration Plugin

In your site's WordPress back office, Go to Plugins >> Add New, search for All in One WP Migration, install and activate it.

In your WordPress menu, hover over All-in-One WP Migration and select Export.

Click on the **Export To** button and choose where to store the backup file.

How to Host Your Website

It's Your Business Address

Store the backup file somewhere that you can access it easily. My preference is to keep it on my local hard disk.

Download the WP Migration Extension

You will need this to restore your backup to the new, empty site that you are about to create on SiteGround.

As it's not available (at the present time) by plugin search, you need to download it onto your hard disk so that you can install it from there.

Go to

https://import.wp-migration.com/

and click the **Download** button under Basic.

This will download a zip file named all-in-one-wp-migration-file-extension.zip.

You won't need this until your new, empty file has been created on SiteGround.

Its purpose is to extend the size of the backup file that can be handled to 512MB.

Large Backup Files

If your backup file is larger than 512MB, you can purchase the PRO version, which allows an unlimited file size.

Create a New Empty Website

Log in to SiteGround

Log in to SiteGround using your normal login credentials.

How to Host Your Website

It's Your Business Address

Then click on WEBSITES.

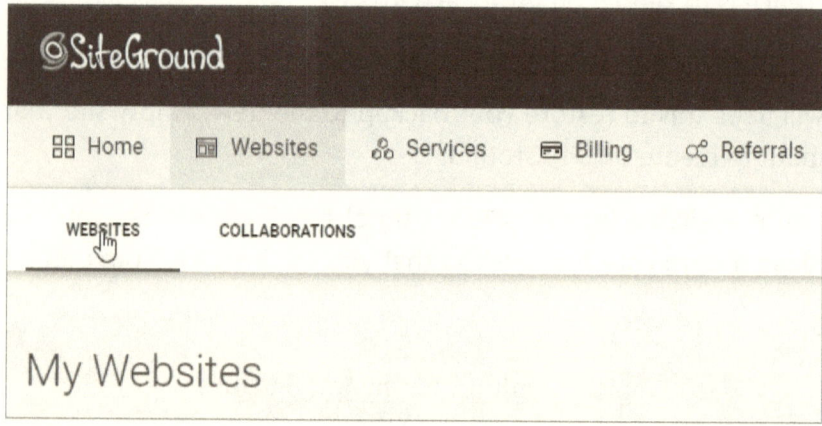

Figure 8: Click on Websites

Then on either **NEW WEBSITE** on the right-hand side.

Figure 9: Click on New Website

or on the **Add New Site** button underneath the list of any existing sites.

How to Host Your Website

It's Your Business Address

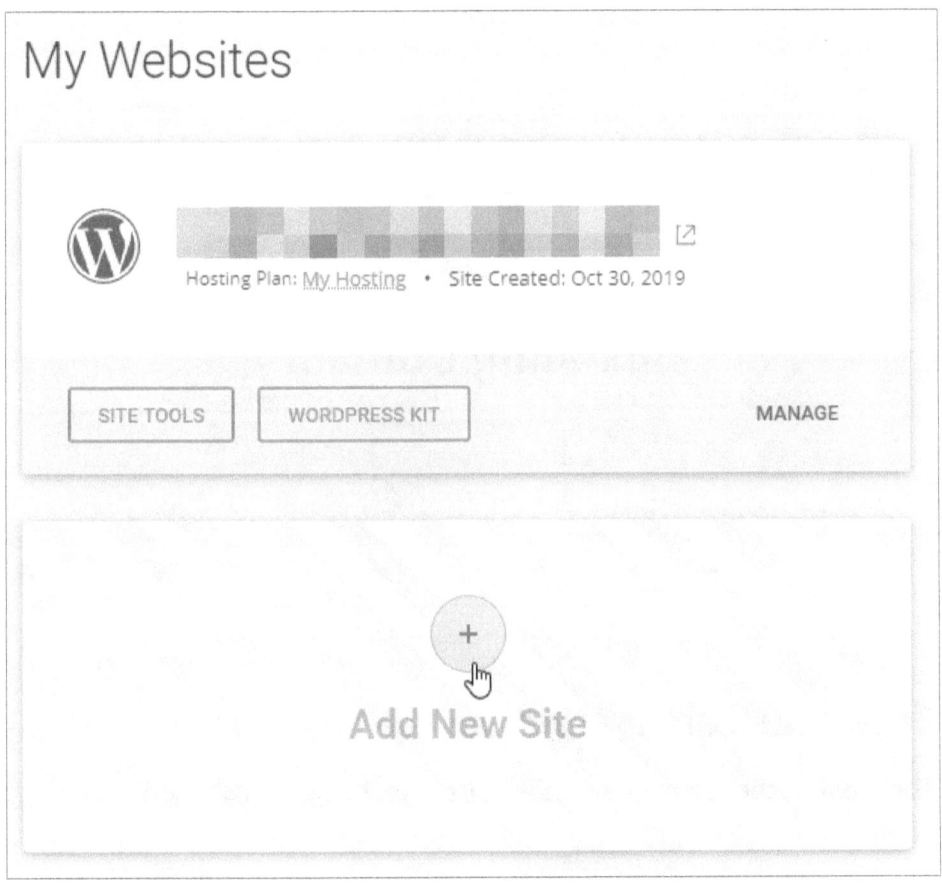

Figure 10: Click on Add New Site

You are using an already registered domain, so click on Select Existing Domain.

How to Host Your Website

It's Your Business Address

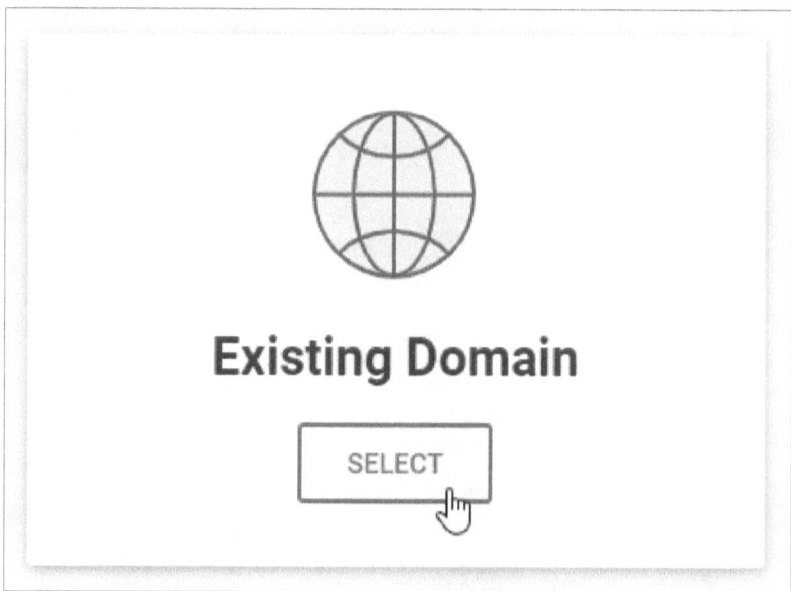

Figure 11: Click on Select Existing Domain

Enter the Domain Name

Then enter the domain name of the site being transferred and press Enter.

How to Host Your Website

It's Your Business Address

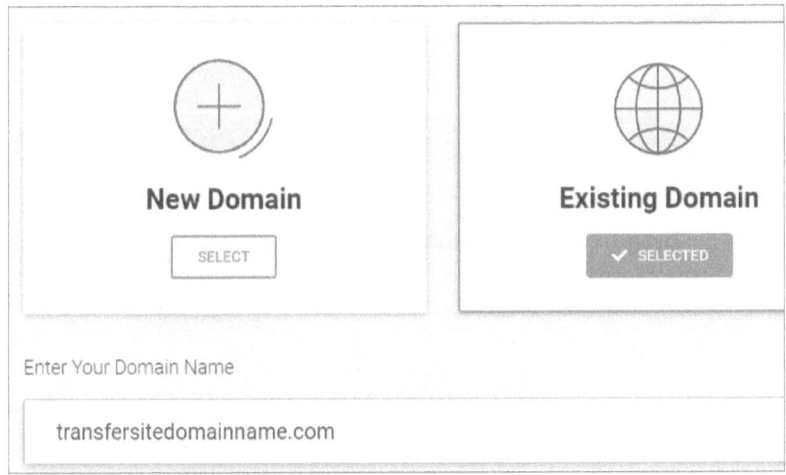

Figure 12: Enter the Domain Name

If your domain name is hosted anywhere other than SiteGround (Namecheap, for example) you will get the following warning message:

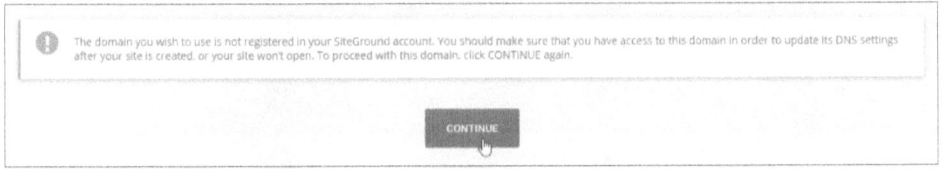

Figure 13: Domain Name Warning

Click the **CONTINUE** button.

You can ignore the Start New Website and Migrate Website options. I'll cover them elsewhere.

Create an Empty Site

For this operation, where you are going to restore our website from a backup, you need to create an empty WordPress site.

How to Host Your Website

It's Your Business Address

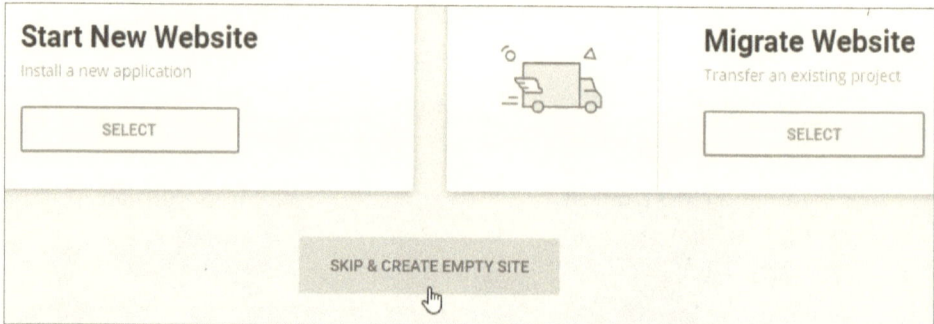

Figure 14: Create New Empty Site

Click on the **SKIP AND CREATE EMPTY SITE** button.

You'll be invited to add the paid SG Site Scanner option. The choice is yours, but it's not essential and can be added later.

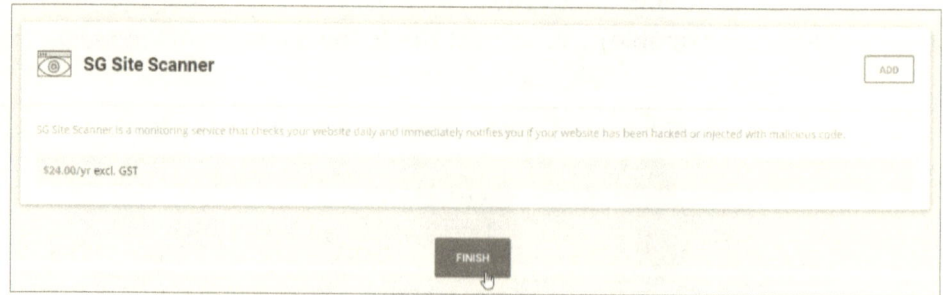

Figure 15: Finish the Installation

Click the **FINISH** button.

You will see a message as SiteGround creates your new, empty website.

How to Host Your Website

It's Your Business Address

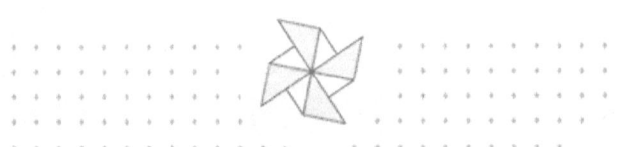

Figure 16: Site Creation Message

After a short time, your site will have been created.

Point the DNS to SiteGround

You will see a screen telling you the SiteGround name servers that are to be used for this site.

How to Host Your Website

It's Your Business Address

Point Your Domain

Please point your domain to the new host server. Your new DNS are:

NS1.US1013.SITEGROUND.US
NS2.US1013.SITEGROUND.US

Read here how to work on a new site before pointing the domain.

Figure 17: The Name Servers to Use for the New Site

In a separate tab, you should now log in to your domain name registrar and update the DNS for this domain name to point to the required name servers.

See Book 3 in my Internet Marketing FAST series *How to Register Your Domain Name* for details of how to do this.

You will also see a screen where you can manage your new site.

How to Host Your Website

It's Your Business Address

Manage the New Site

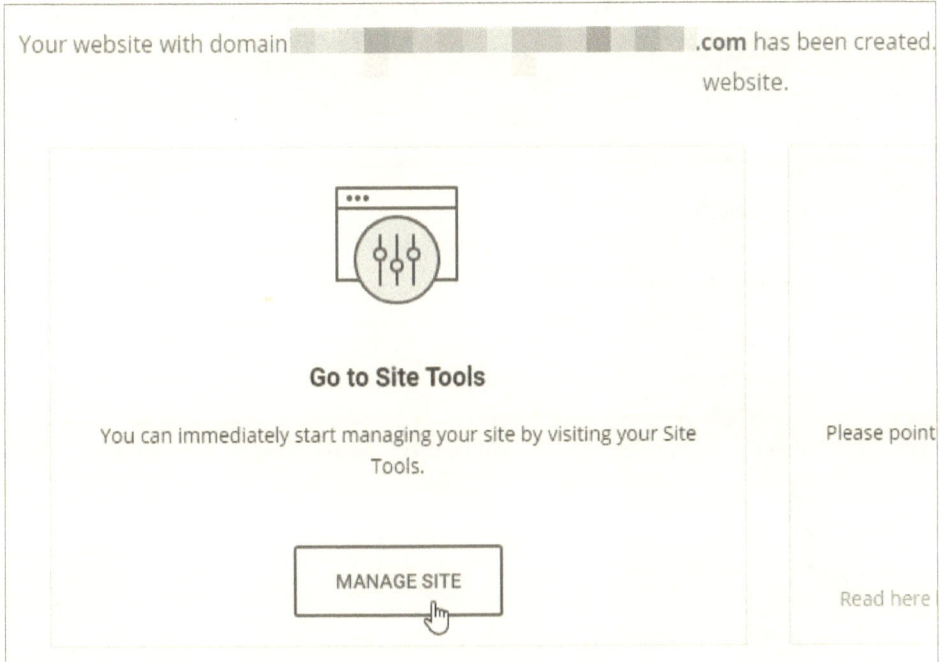

Figure 18: Manage Your New Site

Click on MANAGE SITE.

You will then see a screen showing you many interesting (but fairly irrelevant at this stage) facts about your new website.

You need to install site security and then get into your site's WordPress back office and do the restore from backup.

Install SSL Site Security

Click on SECURITY in the left-hand menu.

31

How to Host Your Website

It's Your Business Address

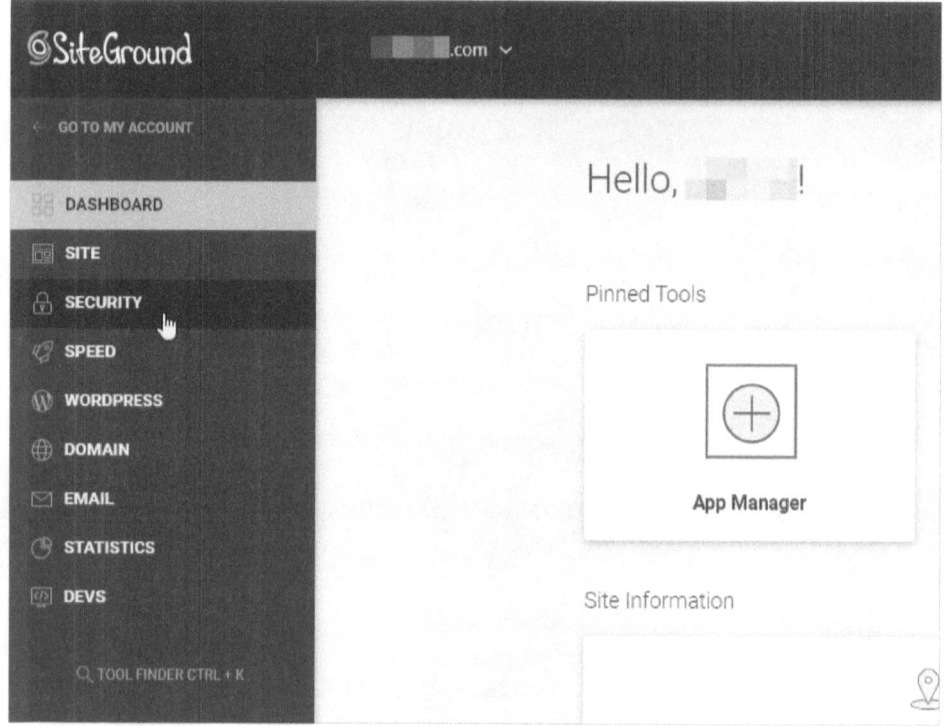

Figure 19: Click on Security

and then on SSL Manager.

How to Host Your Website

It's Your Business Address

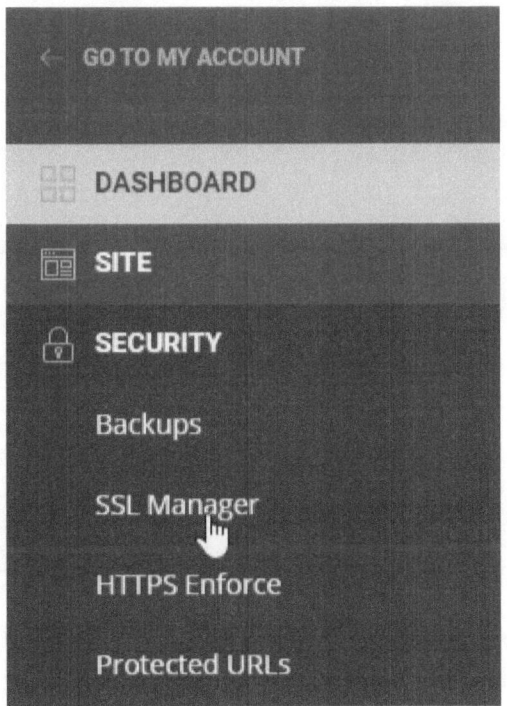

Figure 20: Click on SSL Manager

Then select Let's Encrypt from the drop-down menu.

How to Host Your Website

It's Your Business Address

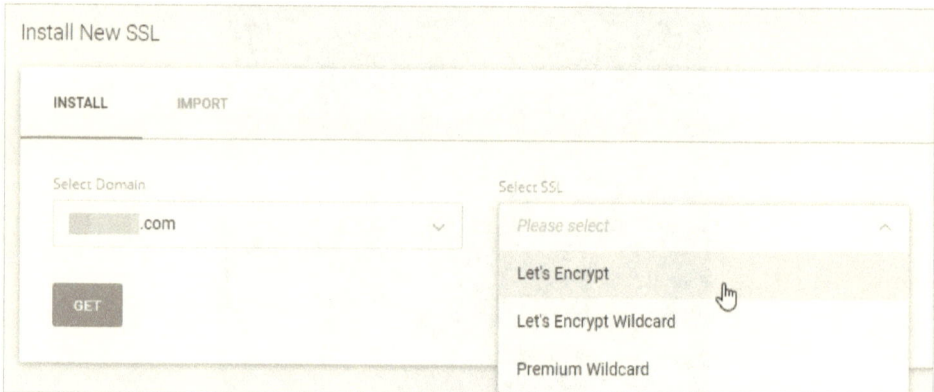

Figure 21: Select Let's Encrypt from the Drop-Down

and then click on the **GET** button.

You will see the message *Your Request is Being Processed*.

Once the Let's Encrypt SSL certificate has been installed, it will appear in the panel underneath.

Sometimes it takes more than one attempt to install the certificate successfully. If you encounter issues, raise a ticket with SiteGround.

How to Host Your Website

It's Your Business Address

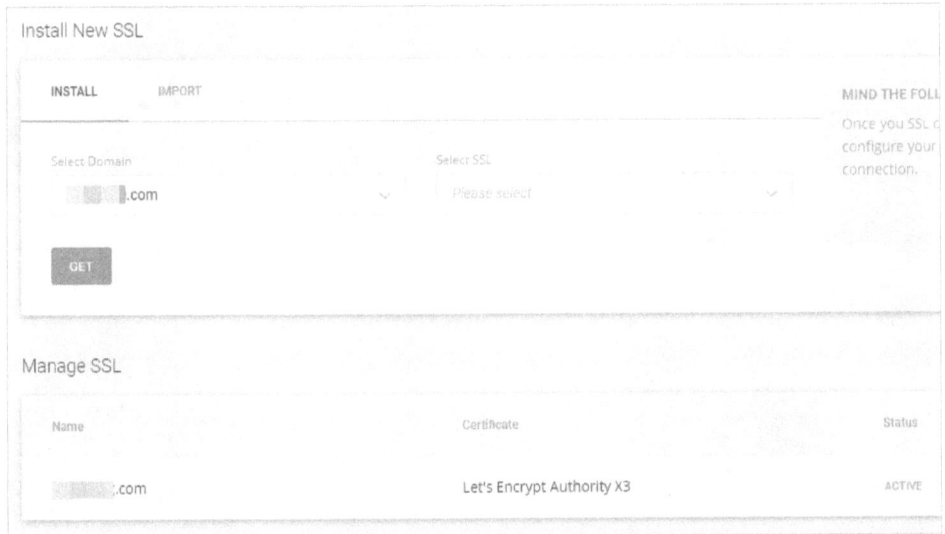

Figure 22: SSL Certificate Installed

Installing Site Security is absolutely essential. It causes your site's URL to start with https:// instead of http://. Without it, you will get warning messages that the site is dangerous when you try to access it and you will not be able to perform some essential functions.

Install WordPress

Now click on WORDPRESS in the left-hand menu.

How to Host Your Website

It's Your Business Address

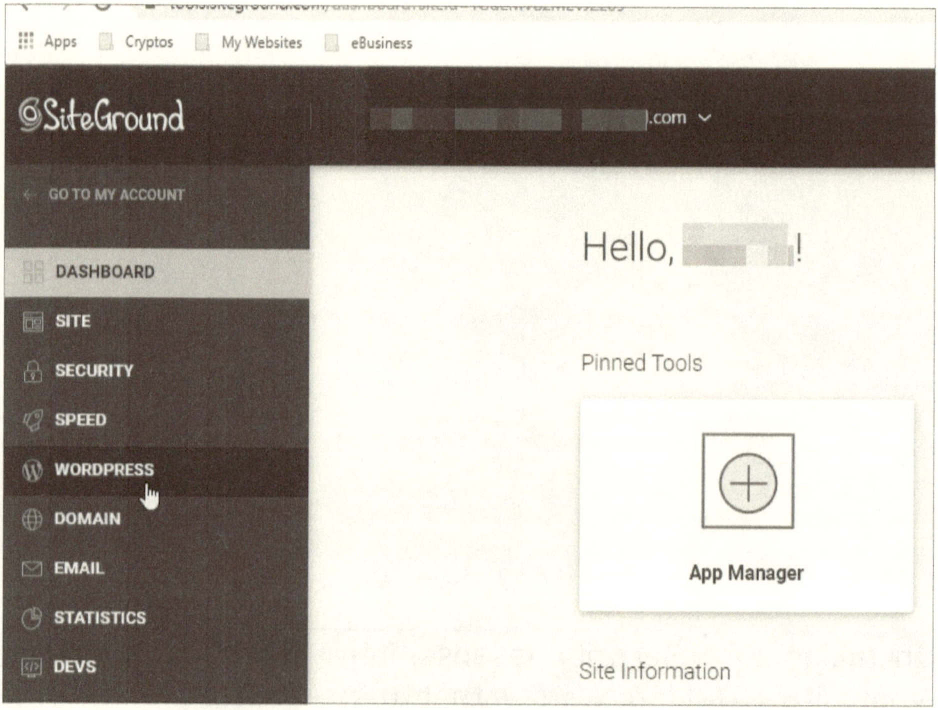

Figure 23: Click on WordPress

Then on Install and Manage.

WORDPRESS

Install & Manage

Staging

Migrator

Figure 24: Install and Manage WordPress

How to Host Your Website

It's Your Business Address

Then select WordPress for Installation.

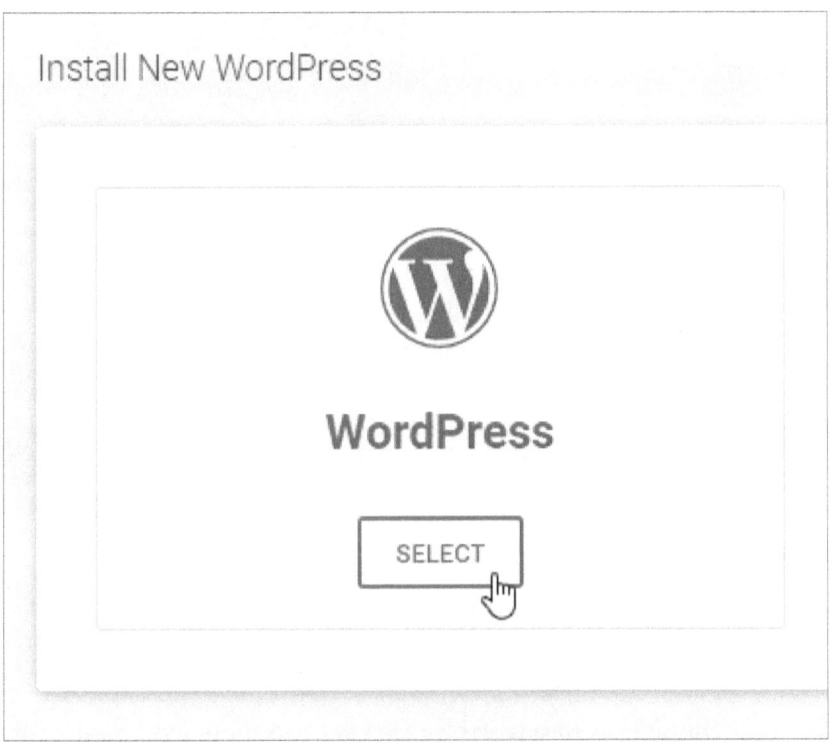

Figure 25: Select WordPress for Installation

You will then see a screen inviting you to enter various items of information for your new WordPress site.

Although you should generate and copy an admin password to use for your initial login, none of this information matters in the long term. Because we will be restoring from a backup, all of the data, including user names and passwords, will be restored from the old site. Also, you can uncheck the box Install with the Starter Plugin.

How to Host Your Website

It's Your Business Address

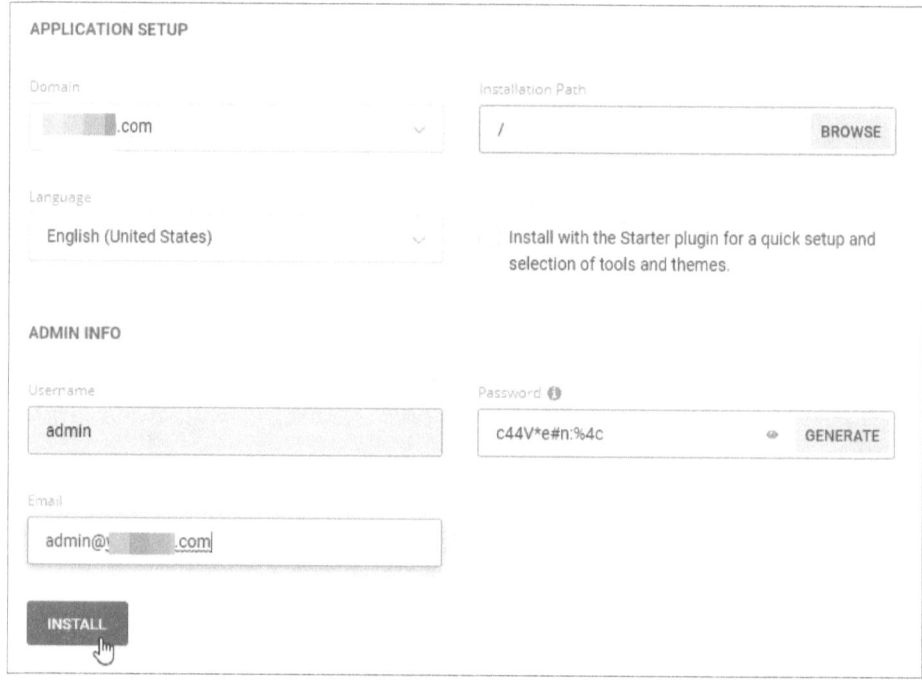

Figure 26: Install WordPress onto Your New Site

You can see the admin password by clicking the View icon next to it. You have to enter an email, but it doesn't need to exist. I just use admin@domainname. Then click INSTALL.

After a short time, your WordPress site will be installed and appear in your site list.

Log in to WP Admin

Click on the right-pointing arrow to log in to the WP Admin panel.

How to Host Your Website

It's Your Business Address

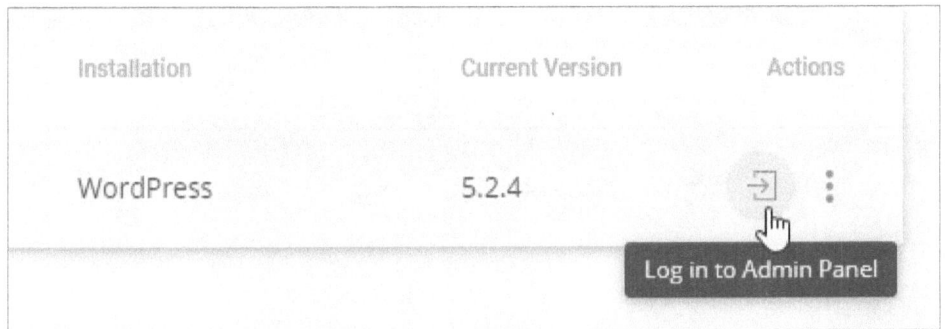

Figure 27: Log into the WP Admin Panel

You'll get a 404 error message at this point if the domain name's DNS isn't pointed at SiteGround's servers. Or even if it is, and propagation hasn't gone far enough yet. All you can do it wait, and keep trying. This isn't a SiteGround issue, it's just how DNS propagation takes place.

Once propagation has reached a certain stage, you'll be able to log in to your WordPress site's back office.

You will then see your new site's WordPress dashboard.

How to Host Your Website

It's Your Business Address

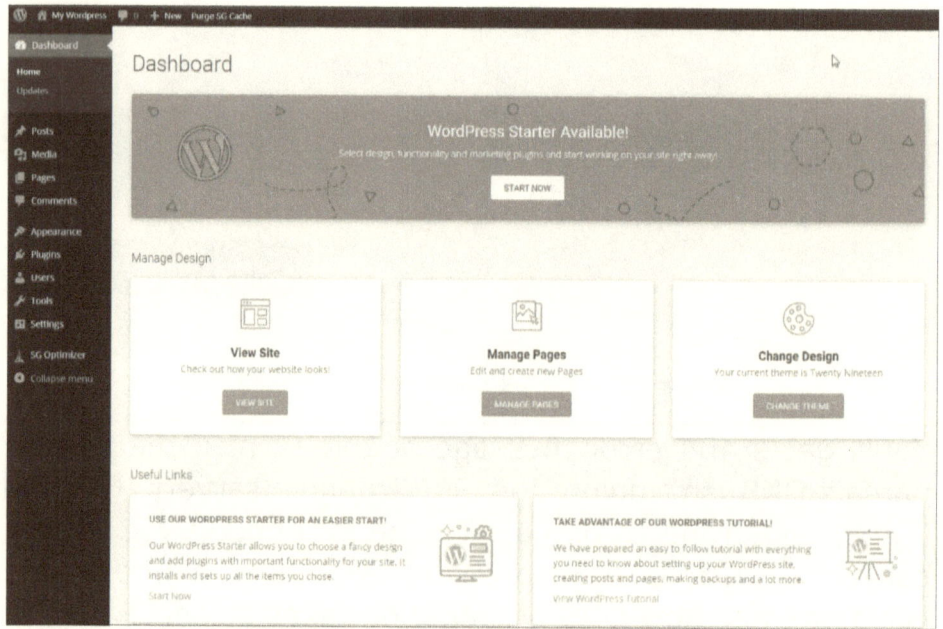

Figure 28: Your WordPress Dashboard

You can ignore everything on here.

Install All in One WP Migration

All you need to do is install the All-in-One WP Migration plugin and the Migration Extensions so that you can restore from the backup you created in Backup the Old Website on page 22

Start by clicking Plugins >> Add New.

How to Host Your Website

It's Your Business Address

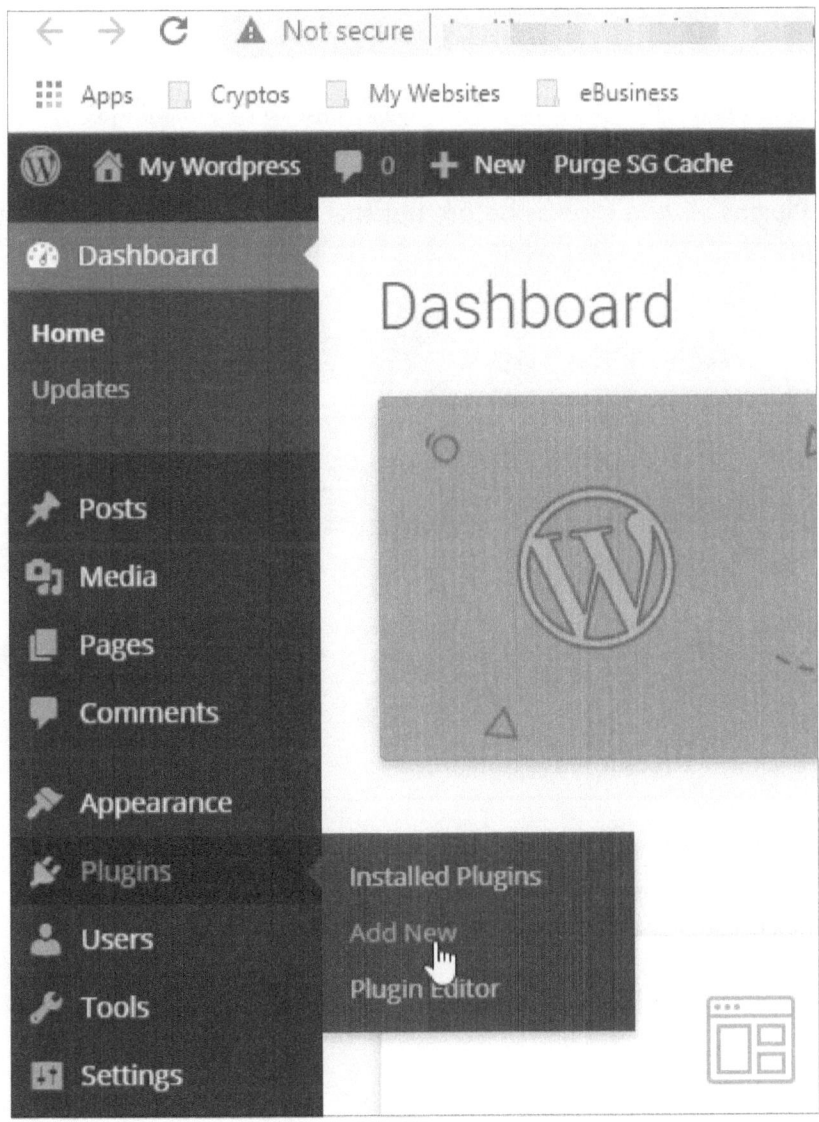

Figure 29: Click Plugins Then Add New

Search for all in one wp migration, then select, install and activate it.

How to Host Your Website

It's Your Business Address

Install WP Migration Extension

You will have downloaded the WP Migration Extension plugin as described in Download the WP Migration Extension on page 23.

Click Plugins >> Add New as before but this time click the **Upload Plugin** button.

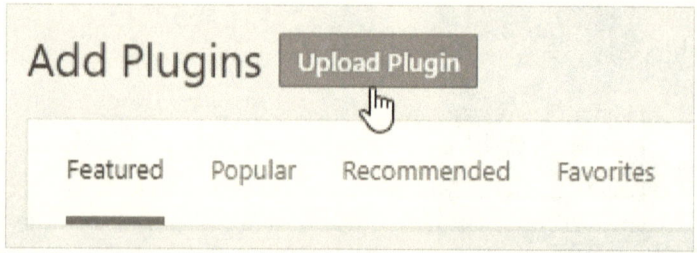

Figure 30: Click Upload Plugin

Then click on Choose File, navigate to the all-in-one-wp-migration-file-extension zip file that you downloaded and double click on it.

Then click the **Install Now** button.

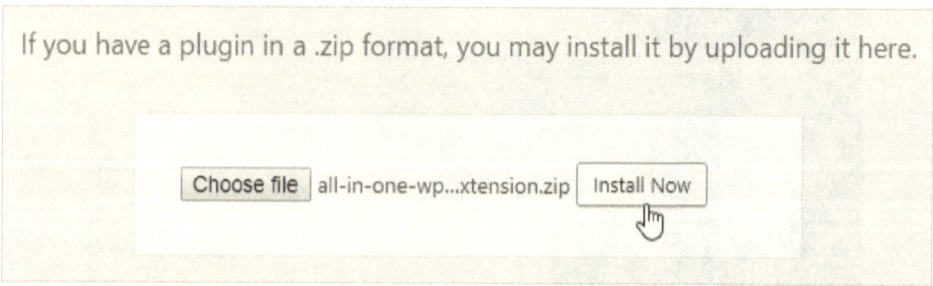

Figure 31: Install the WP Migration Extension

Then activate the installed plugin.

How to Host Your Website

It's Your Business Address

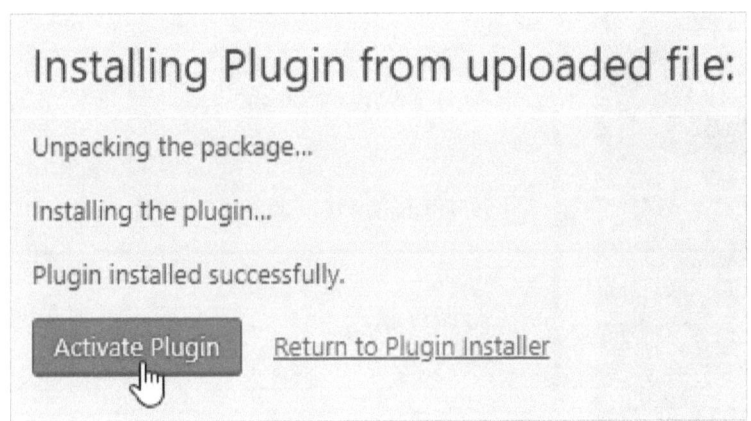

Figure 32: Activate the Plugin

With the plugin installed and activated, you can now import from a backup file under 512MB.

If your backup file exceeds 512MB, refer to Large Backup Files on page 23.

Restore from Backup

Hover over All-in-One WP Migration in the WordPress menu and select Import.

How to Host Your Website

It's Your Business Address

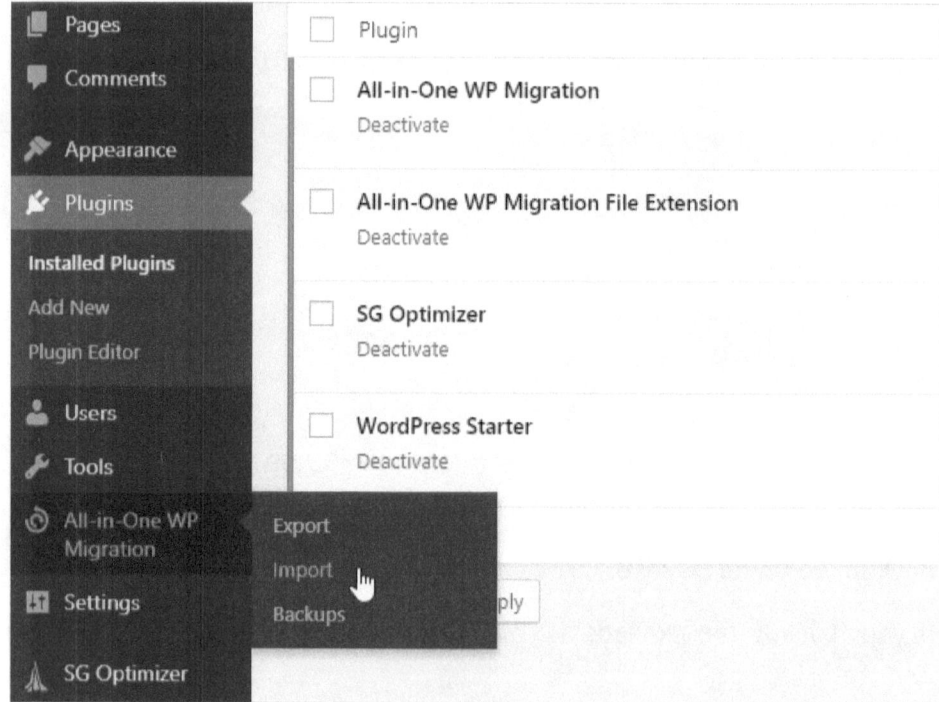

Figure 33: Select All in One WP Migration Import

Select where your backup file has been stored. If you've stored it on your local hard disk, select FILE.

How to Host Your Website

It's Your Business Address

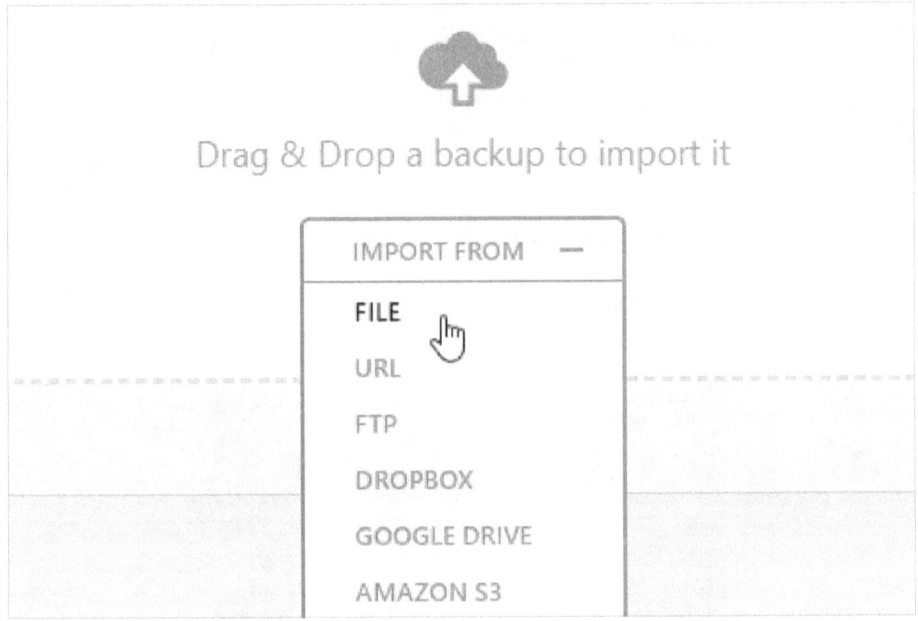

Figure 34: Select the Import Source

Navigate to where you stored the backup file and double-click on it.

The import will start and you'll see a progress message.

How to Host Your Website

It's Your Business Address

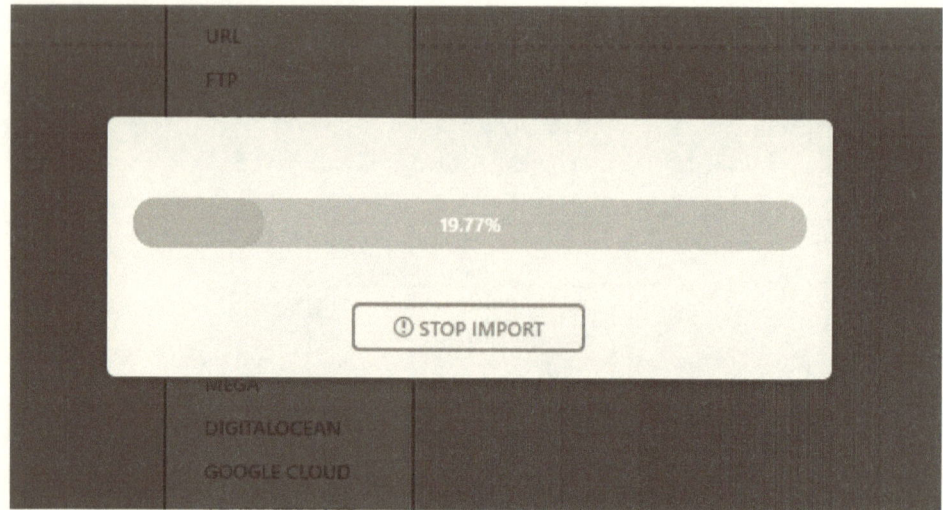

Figure 35: Import Progress Bar

Import takes longer than export. Be prepared.

When import is complete, you'll see a screen warning you that proceeding will overwrite the target site.

This is exactly what you want to happen.

How to Host Your Website

It's Your Business Address

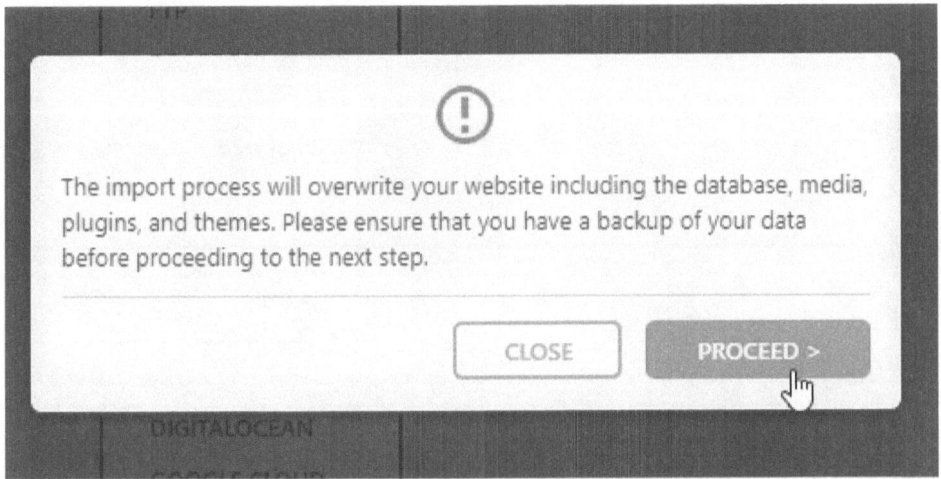

Figure 36: Proceed with the Import Process

Click PROCEED.

You should see a message telling you that your file has imported successfully.

For some reason, the site's permalink structure doesn't get carried across, so you need to fix this.

You will probably have to log in to do this. Because your old site has now been imported, you'll use its login credentials.

How to Host Your Website

It's Your Business Address

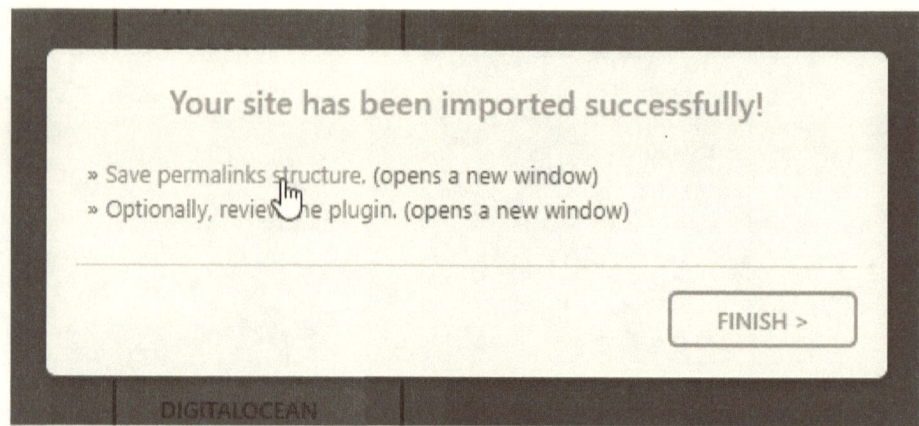

Figure 37: Fix the Permalinks Structure

Click **Save permalinks structure (opens a new window)** make sure that **Post Name** is selected and click **Save Changes.**

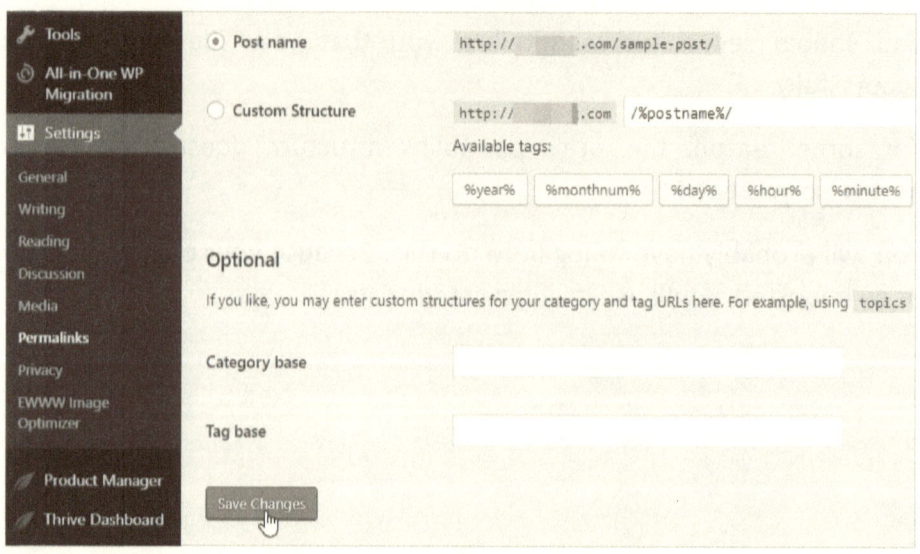

Figure 38: Permalink Setting

How to Host Your Website

It's Your Business Address

Return to the SiteGround window and click Finish to complete the import.

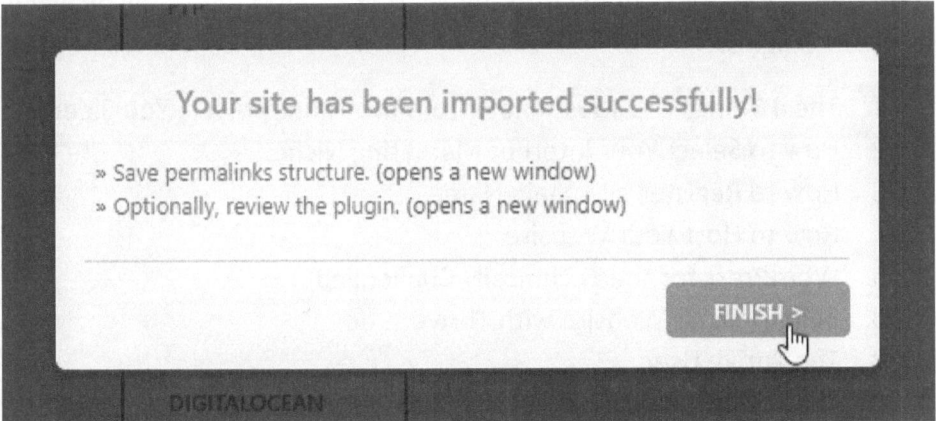

Figure 39: Click Finish to Complete the Import

And that's it!

Your new site should now be exactly as your previous site, but running on SiteGround.

This includes your user names and passwords.

How to Host Your Website
It's Your Business Address

The Rest of the Books

Here are all the books in my Internet Marketing FAST series, all available as Kindle Singles.

1. The 4 Things You Must Know (to Make Money While You Sleep)
2. How to Select Your Internet Marketing Niche
3. How to Register a Domain Name
4. How to Host Your Website
5. WordPress for the Technically Challenged
6. Building Your Website with Thrive
7. The Thrive User
8. The Thrive Expert
9. Become an Affiliate Marketing Ninja
10. Become an E-Commerce Ninja
11. The Deadly Combo of Blog Posts and Landing Pages
12. Google is Your New Best Friend
13. Building Your Mailing List
14. All About Free and Paid Traffic
15. How to Publish Your Book on Amazon
16. The Secret to Making Money with Your Internet Businesses (after You've Done Everything Else)

You can get the Kindle and Paperback links to the books on Amazon at

https://superaffiliatechallenge.com/internet-marketing-fast-books-from-amazon/

How to Host Your Website

It's Your Business Address

About the Author

As a 76 year old fitness fanatic and successful internet marketer, Phil Lancaster is a bit of an anomaly.

Through a combination of bad luck and bad business decisions, he found himself broke and alone at 74.

Now, a year and a bit later, he has several internet businesses that combine to bring him a 6-figure income.

It wasn't easy and he got burned a few times on the way, but he reckons that anyone can do it with the right road map.

He wants to help you to get started the way he did, but without making the same mistakes.

Anyone, from student to baby boomer (and older) can make money through the internet.

Phil's IM Fast series of mini-books will get you started. At just $2.99 each, you won't find a better investment.